WITHDRAWN

P9-DKF-943

Martin de Porres

the rose in the desert

written by
Gary D. Schmidt

iLLustrated by
David Diaz

LANSDALE PUBLIC LIBRARY
301 VINE STREET
LANSDALE, PA 19446

CLARION BOOKS
HOUGHTON MIFFLIN HARCOURT
BOSTON • NEW YORK

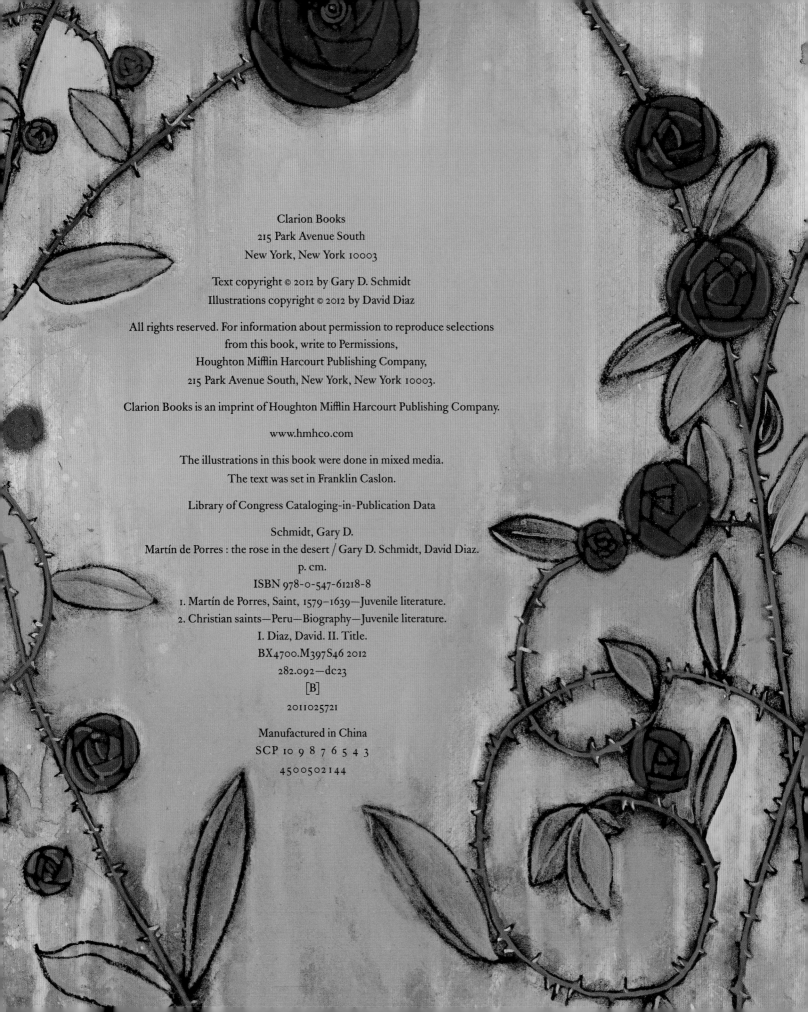

Clarion Books
215 Park Avenue South
New York, New York 10003

Text copyright © 2012 by Gary D. Schmidt
Illustrations copyright © 2012 by David Diaz

All rights reserved. For information about permission to reproduce selections
from this book, write to Permissions,
Houghton Mifflin Harcourt Publishing Company,
215 Park Avenue South, New York, New York 10003.

Clarion Books is an imprint of Houghton Mifflin Harcourt Publishing Company.

www.hmhco.com

The illustrations in this book were done in mixed media.
The text was set in Franklin Caslon.

Library of Congress Cataloging-in-Publication Data

Schmidt, Gary D.
Martín de Porres : the rose in the desert / Gary D. Schmidt, David Diaz.
p. cm.
ISBN 978-0-547-61218-8
1. Martín de Porres, Saint, 1579–1639—Juvenile literature.
2. Christian saints—Peru—Biography—Juvenile literature.
I. Diaz, David. II. Title.
BX4700.M397S46 2012
282.092—dc23
[B]
2011025721

Manufactured in China
SCP 10 9 8 7 6 5 4 3
4500502144

For Bill Vande Kopple and Elizabeth Vander Lei

—G.D.S.

For Lin Oliver and Stephen Mooser,

the lamp, lifeboat, and ladder to so many

—D.D.

aNNA VELÁZQUEZ hurried out of the *barrios* of Lima
and onto the plaza. She carried a quiet baby, wrapped closely
so that no one could see him—but no one was looking.

The slave boys sweeping the plaza saw only the dusty cobblestones.

The Spanish royals sipping lemon ices saw only their ruby rings.

And the priests standing on the cathedral steps saw only another
beggar, and turned away.

5

Anna carried the baby into the cool dark of the cathedral. But when the priest unwrapped him, he frowned. "Is the child's father Spanish?" he asked.

Anna's heart beat quickly.

"And you are African," he said.

Anna nodded.

The priest frowned again. The baby's father was a royal conqueror. His mother was a slave.

The baby looked up at him with dark eyes.

"Who is this child?" asked the priest.

"He is a rose in the desert," said Anna.

The priest frowned even more. The baby would have no name to be remembered. He would live by sweeping the cobblestones of the plaza, or selling lemon ices to the royals, or begging on the cathedral steps. So the priest dipped his hand into the holy water. "I baptize you, the son of an unknown father."

"I will call him Martín," said Anna.

But the priest still frowned.

Martín grew up with his sister, Juana, in the *barrios*, where slaves and the poorest Indians lived. On hot summer days, they went to the rooftop to escape the stink of the leatherworks. On rainy days, the River Rímac flooded its banks, so that cold water—and sometimes rats—poured into their house. Hunger lived in their home. Illness was their companion.

When Martín was eight, his father, Don Juan de Porres, came from faraway Ecuador to see his children for the first time. He could not bear the stink and cold and hunger and illness of the *barrios*. He took Martín and Juana back with him. He gave them his name.

The royals and the priests of Ecuador frowned.

When Martín grew older, Don Juan apprenticed him to a *cirujano* back in Lima. "You will learn to take out teeth, to bleed a patient with leeches, to set broken bones, and to cut hair," the *cirujano* told him.

The royals and the priests of Lima frowned.

Then one day, a bleeding man stumbled to the *cirujano*'s house when only Martín the apprentice was there. "Mongrel, find the doctor!" he cried. But Martín cleaned the wound and bandaged it with his own hands. The man marveled.

"Who is this strange boy?" he asked.

After he had healed, the man brought the seeds of a lemon tree as a gift. That night, Martín and Juana scooped a hole behind their house, and Martín planted the seeds. In the morning, a tree had spread its branches, and from every branch, a lemon hung. From then on, there were always lemons—in spring, summer, fall, and even in winter.

The neighbors plucked the fruit and asked, "Who is this strange boy?"

Word spread of the apprentice with the healing hands and the wonderful lemon tree. "It could not be true," said the royals on Lima's plaza. "It is not possible," said the priests in the cool cathedral. But the slave boys sweeping the dusty cobblestones said, "Could it be?" And the Indians of the *barrios* begging on the cathedral steps asked, "Is it possible?"

When Martín was fifteen, he knocked on the doors of the Monastery of the Holy Rosary. Father Lorenzana, the prior, frowned. "You are not of pure blood," he said. "You can never be a priest."

Martín smiled. "I will wash the dishes and tunics," he said. "I will clean the halls and baths. I will tend the gardens and mules." He looked at the prior with dark eyes.

Who is this strange boy? Father Lorenzana wondered. But Father Lorenzana gave him a white tunic and a black cape, and Martín began his new life.

Every day after Prime, Martín washed the floors of the brothers' cells. After Terce, he cut their tonsured hair. For the prayers at Nones, he opened the monastery doors so that the brothers might walk inside in silence. After Vespers, he swept the holy chapel. And whenever the brothers called, he came.

"Son of a slave!" they said.

"You know who I am," said Martín.

But they did not.

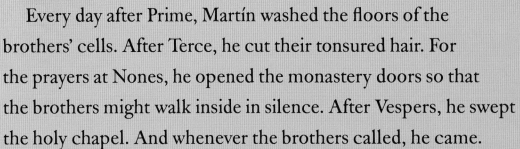

Then Father Lorenzana began to hear tales: Stubborn mules in the stables stretched their necks to Martín. Pecking chickens in the hen houses begged to be stroked as he reached for their eggs. Greedy mice in the barn stopped raiding the kitchen and took grain from Martín's hand.

Then Father Lorenzana heard more than tales.

After Martín healed a wounded dog that had limped to the monastery, more beaten and starved dogs crawled to him from all over Lima. Under Martín's tender hands, they came back to barking life. Father Lorenzana could not hear the church bells over their barking.

"Martín!" he cried.

So Martín brought the dogs home, and they panted in the shade of the wonderful lemon tree.

Soon, all the people of the *barrios* knew who the young *cirujano* was. When a man was hurt, he was carried to Martín. When a child grew pale, she was brought to Martín. When a slave was whipped, he staggered to Martín. And when the infirmary of the monastery was filled with the poorest, Martín carried his patients to play with the panting dogs in the shade of the wonderful lemon tree.

Soon the brothers in the monastery asked him to doctor them, too. He washed their sores. He spooned them soup. He healed their wounds. Some said he walked through locked doors to cool a fever with a drink.

When the Spanish royals heard, they sent for Martín to care for them, too. And they learned to wait for him to tend the poorest among the *barrios* first.

After thirteen years, every soul in Lima knew who Martín was: Not a mongrel. Not the son of a slave. "He is a rose in the desert," they said.

So Martín stood in the chapter room of the monastery and made his vows. Father Lorenzana leaned down and kissed him: "Now you are our brother," he said.

And the stories became more wonderful than before. Some said that
Martín could appear in two places at the same time. Others saw angels
with lighted candles guiding him through the halls. Along the River
Rímac, the lemon and orange trees he planted gave harvests all year
long. And when he appeared with bread in the *barrios* or in the red-tiled
mansions, it was always enough.

That is how it was for forty-five years, until
one day, Martín put on a new tunic and went
to his bed. The brothers gathered around him.
"Martín," they whispered. "Martín."

He smiled. "Maybe I will be more
useful there than here," he said.

His brothers began to sing.

Their sweet song drifted from the
monastery.

Across Lima's plaza, the sweeping slave boys and the Spanish royals and the Indians of the *barrios* and the priests of the cathedral listened, and they began to sing.

When Martín heard their song, he smiled.

And while all the people of Lima, standing hand in hand, sang, Martín closed his dark eyes.

Note

Martín de Porres was born in Lima, Peru, on December 9, 1579. His childhood was one of neglect and poverty, but after his education in Ecuador and his entrance into the Dominican monastery in Lima, his life became one of compassion and charity. His humility and service are symbolized by the broom with which he is usually pictured. But his greatest gift was his ability to ignore the boundaries his world had erected and to reach toward the poor and the ignored. When he died on November 3, 1639, he immediately became a figure of tremendous appeal for those in Peru who had resigned themselves to a hopeless life of oppression. He was beatified in 1837 and canonized in May 1962—the first black saint in the Americas—when Pope John XXIII named him the patron saint of universal brotherhood. He soon also became the patron saint of interracial relations, social justice, those of mixed race, public education, and animal shelters.

WITHDRAWN

LANSDALE PUBLIC LIBRARY
301 VINE STREET
LANSDALE, PA 19446
June - 2018